# Dou

## Exploring Richard
## Assurance and Salvation

**Andrea Russell**
Director of Formation for Ministry, Diocese of Oxford

**GROVE BOOKS LIMITED**
**RIDLEY HALL RD CAMBRIDGE CB3 9HU**

# Contents





**First Impression** May 2021
**ISSN** 2633-8394
**ISBN** 978 1 78827 124 0

# Introduction

# 1

How certain does Christian belief need to be? Is doubt the enemy of faith?

As I began to write this booklet, I realized that I cannot recall a sermon on doubt, or in fact one on how certain faith should be or must be. Does this mean that this is not a topic anyone thinks about anymore? Do we just assume that everyone sitting next to us in church has a strong faith? For those of us who preach regularly, maybe we see our role as building up faith rather than engaging with doubt and questions.

I then began to wonder whether, in certain circles, there is more concern about *what* we believe rather than *how* we hold to that belief. There is, I think, still the idea that if we believe the right things, we will inevitably know for certain that this is truth through the Holy Spirit's power and revelation. In my experience, as a tutor in theology, I have overheard conversations that suggest some of this. I once overheard two young men discussing Jesus' resurrection and one boldly declared that for those who wanted to be certain about this, the evidence was there, and that not to believe it was an act of wilful sinfulness. It seems that in some parts of the Christian tradition the notion of certainty is very much alive and kicking.

Further delving revealed that this is not an area that is often spoken about or even written about. There are areas of theology and practice that are very much in vogue: mission, of course, but also others, such as the ministry of the laity, apologetics and hospitality. Explorations of doubt and certainty are not hot topics, although there have been some recent publications in this area such as Anthony Thiselton's *Doubt, Faith and Certainty*, Graham Ward's *Unbelievable* and Alex Wright's *Exploring Doubt*.[1] Questions of doubt and uncertainty do, though, often arise in classroom discussions, and implicitly when enquirers' groups, such as *Alpha*, are spoken of. When Dave Tomlinson suggested that spiritual certainty may not be good for us,[2] Ian Paul responded in his blog to suggest that God wants us to be delivered from one kind of certainty (the bad sort) into another kind of certainty (the right sort) which he equates to confidence.[3] Questions of faith and doubt, assurance, certainty and confidence seem still to be with us.

**Explorations of doubt and certainty are not hot topics**

John Humphreys, the well-known broadcaster, has engaged with questions of faith and doubt over many years. In his book, *In God We Doubt* he puts forward an argument that both strident atheism and certain faith are often easier to hold to than an honest doubting, questioning form of belief. It is only in the latter, he claims, that experience and doctrine truly engage with each other. In his conversation with Rowan Williams, Humphreys draws attention to the human cost woven within many of the arguments Christians rely on to answer questions raised by evil and suffering. This leaves him with too many questions and doubts, he says, for him to assent to Christian faith.[4] This seems unfortunate, as Humphreys' concerns resonate for many Christians. Does this mean that they also have a weak faith or maybe even show themselves to have no real faith at all? Are they, too, effectively agnostic?

All of this leads us to ask some questions about faith. Setting aside, as much as we can, what constitutes the true *content* of faith, are we required as Christians to hold our beliefs with a high or complete degree of *certainty*? When does weak faith become faithlessness? Is there a difference between confidence and certainty? Is assurance simply the same word as certainty or does it mean something different? Is doubt an enemy of faith that needs to be extinguished?

This may seem like quite a list of questions, but they are crucial if we want to open up an honest conversation about faith with each other and with those outside of and on the fringes of the church.

It may come as no surprise that we are not the only people who have considered these questions. In fact, they have been explored many times and in different ways over the centuries. There is one era of Christian history, however, the sixteenth century, when faith and doubt were hugely significant topics. Exploring this period shows that the debates were not simply theoretical, they had serious consequences for the lives of many Christians. As such, this seems a good place for us to dig deeper.

# Does Faith Need to be Certain? A Sixteenth-century Dilemma

# 2

The sixteenth century is surely one of the most exciting, challenging and shameful periods in Christian history. England began the century as a Roman Catholic country; its religious life was in step with Rome and Christian beliefs evolved and developed in line with Roman Catholic teaching and tradition (at least on the surface). As the century drew to a close English society had been transformed. The English Reformation, echoing the Continental upheaval and yet retaining and developing its own unique identity, resulted in England leaving the century as a Protestant country, no longer under the authority of the Pope and with the monarch as the Supreme Governor of the Church of England. What lay ahead was further tumult and division, and whether this was seen as progress and liberation or tragedy and fragmentation (or indeed a mixture of both) depends upon our own views and beliefs.

But amidst all of this political and ecclesial tumult a particular theological fire was burning, fuelled by questions as to certainty of belief and assurance of salvation. The embers had been lit almost accidentally. At the heart of the Reformation had been the stand against what was seen as the power of the Roman Catholic Church to control and limit God's salvation, or at least the perception that this was possible. The Reformers viewed the church's teaching as a belief in merit and works as the basis for God's acceptance. They saw this as inevitably leading to anxiety and a doubt-filled hope that robbed Christians of their birthright. Could you ever be sure you had done enough?

**Could you ever be sure you had done enough?**

It is clear that some of the Reformers' views were based on an unnuanced reading of Catholic theology and practice, misunderstanding (or ignoring) the pivotal role of grace. Nevertheless, their critique led them to declare that Christians could experience a certainty of faith refocused on God's gracious salvation.

In her essay, 'Faith and Assurance,' Debra Shuger draws our attention to Phillip Melanchthon, a close ally of Martin Luther, whose writing provides us with a clear example of this view. Drawing on Melanchthon's *Commentary on Romans*, written in 1532, she comments that for this Magisterial Reformer 'The certainty of faith stands over and against the Roman church's teaching that our acceptance by God is contingent upon works and therefore inescapably uncertain.'[5] But even more interesting is her direct quote from him (using her own translation from the German) that 'God can neither be truly worshipped nor adored unless…our minds are freed from doubt.'[6]

This theology of certainty and assurance became linked to many of the facets of Reformation theology and especially to the doctrine of predestination. Again, this doctrine (shared by Roman Catholics but reinterpreted by the Reformers) was intended to deliver peace and comfort to all Christians. By highlighting God's choosing of us rather than our rather presumptuous idea that we could choose God, the Reformers sought to teach that God's grace is supremely unfathomable and powerful and on this we can rely. Salvation is from first to last an act of God. God elects those who are to be saved; he calls them and gives them faith as a gift. Justification is not earned but given freely and it is Christ's righteousness that is central here, imputed to the believer through that gift of faith. Sanctification, the outworking of God's grace in the believer's life, is a gift and work of the Holy Spirit and, through the further gift of perseverance, the believer will at last see the face of God in the bliss of eternity.

This desire to comfort and reassure lay at the heart of Reformed theology and was seen clearly in the *ordo salutis,* the golden chain of salvation, based on Romans 8.28–30:

> We know that all things work together for good for those who love God, who are called according to his purpose. For those whom he foreknew he also predestined to be conformed to the image of his Son, in order that he might be the firstborn within a large family. And those whom he predestined he also called; and those whom he called he also justified; and those whom he justified he also glorified.[7]

The burden of anxious wondering, the Reformers argued, was lifted as this teaching illuminated God's desire and ability to save and the fathomless and glorious depth of God's mercy and grace. Each link of the chain gave strength to the other, being so 'coupled and knit together, that if you hold fast one lincke, you draw unto you the whole chaine; if you let goe one, you loose all.'[8] Assurance was the product of participation in this golden chain of salvation and thus a precious gift in the life of the believer.

> To wrongly think that one could not attain assurance of salvation was a great hindrance to the Christian life, and therefore, the spiritual writers agreed, the doctrine of assurance must be taught to all, so that they might know themselves to be 'beloved of God.'[9]

Whilst preachers communicated this belief and assurance in many different ways, the core was the same and its aim was to deliver the downtrodden, anxious people of God from the snares of the devil. Satan wanted them to live their lives in fear and uncertainty. Instead, they would enter into the glorious freedom of the children of God, where gift and grace replaced work and merit.

The intention was good. Delivering people from the fear of whether they are good enough or had done enough to be loved by God is surely one of the key benefits of the gospel. But there was of course a problem. How did you know that you had been called? Once this was clear, the work of the golden chain could be relied upon. But how could you be certain that this applied to you?

Even from this brief overview it is not difficult to see that those who were the least proud, the more fragile in faith and prone to doubt and question may not find assurance, but concern, in this declaration of grace. This teaching might well challenge the lofty and over-confident, but it did not differentiate between the arrogant and the fearful. In the same way, those who claimed certainty and assurance (and these words came to be used interchangeably) may well have been doing so outwardly, whilst inwardly living lives of doubt and desperation.

## Calvin's Contribution

One of the giants of the Reformation is, of course, John Calvin. Born in France in 1509, a Roman Catholic and a lawyer, he became one of the most influential thinkers and preachers of his day. After leaving the Roman Catholic Church in the 1530s he became a champion of the Reformation and his theological views still reverberate down the centuries.

**Calvin believed that faith and salvation are God's gifts to us**

Like all protestant reformers, Calvin believed that faith and salvation are God's gifts to us. His *Institutes of the Christian Religion*, originally written in 1536 and updated during his lifetime, help us to grasp the importance of this question of certainty and the nature of faith for those living through such turbulent times. In chapter II of Book III, Calvin explains the human condition and God's plan of gracious liberation and rescue, namely 'the appearance of Christ the Redeemer,' adding the words 'if indeed, with firm faith we embrace this mercy and rest in it with steadfast hope.'[10] Those words, 'firm faith' are important. What does it mean to have a firm faith?

A little later in the same chapter Calvin explores this question. He links faith securely with the word and describes believers as those who hear the word of God as disclosing to us God's will for us. Calvin's argument here is quite complex, but he is struggling to explore and explain the idea that faith is more than simply assenting to the church's teaching, or a vague feeling, but instead is rooted in Scripture in a way that allows the word to read us and reveal God's will to us for our lives. But still the question of how certain you need to be hovers in the background and Calvin circles back to this again and again. In this longer quotation we begin to see that firm faith is, for Calvin, a certain faith.

> Now therefore, we hold faith to be a knowledge of God's will toward us, perceived from his Word. But the foundation of this is a preconceived conviction of God's truth. As for its certainty so long as your mind is at war with itself, the Word will be of doubtful and weak authority or rather of none. And it is not enough to believe that God is trustworthy who can neither deceive nor lie unless you hold to be beyond doubt that whatever proceeds from him is sacred and inviolable truth.[11]

Whilst Calvin seeks to engage with our sinfulness and the difficulties we face regarding faith, his constant refrain is one of certainty, sureness and firmness.[12] Weak faith, though, is still faith, he says, and this must have brought comfort and joy to those who struggled to believe. But in other passages this seems less evident.

> For, as faith is not content with a doubtful and changeable opinion, so it is not content with an obscure and confused conception; but requires full and fixed certainty such as men are wont to have from things experienced and proved.[13]

As Calvin moved on to consider the question of perseverance (a key part of the golden chain) this reassurance became less obvious. If perseverance is the true test of faith, and if we see others fall away who seemed to have had great faith, how can we be sure that this will not happen to us? Calvin faces this question head on and realizes that it is a deeply pastoral one, for such worries in effect rob us of any comfort.

> Thus, they say that even though according to our present state of righteousness we can judge concerning our possession of the grace of God, the knowledge of final perseverance remains in suspense. A fine confidence of salvation is left to us, if by moral conjecture we judge that at the present moment we are in grace, but we know not what will become of us tomorrow.[14]

But Calvin's full answer is perhaps less than helpful as he simply goes on to quote Romans 8.38–39:

> I am surely convinced that neither angels, nor powers, nor principalities, nor death, nor life, nor things present, nor things to come...will separate us from the love by which the Lord embraces us in Christ.[15]

What follows might highlight for us the depth of the problem here:

> For though only those predestined to salvation receive the light of faith and truly feel the power of the gospel, yet experience shows that the reprobate are sometimes affected by almost the same feeling as the elect, so that even in their own judgment they do not in any way differ from the elect (*cf* Acts 13.48). Therefore it is not at all absurd that the apostle should attribute to them a taste of the heavenly gifts (Heb 6.4–6)—and Christ, faith for a time (Luke 8.13) not because they firmly grasp the force of spiritual grace and the sure light of faith, but because the Lord to render them more convicted and inexcusable, steals into their minds to the extent that his goodness may be tasted without the Spirit of adoption.[16]

Whilst Calvin writes much more nuanced passages about certainty, faith and doubt, it is not difficult to see how those with an already fragile faith might find this teaching anxiety-producing.

## A Possible Way Forward

One of the answers given in this highly sensitive and complex area was to encourage those who were concerned to take a different approach. The advice was, in effect, not to start at the beginning of the chain but in the middle and to work backwards. Individuals were encouraged to sift their lives and look for evidence of the Spirit's work, the process of sanctification. To an extent external conduct could be a guide. The fruits of the Spirit—love, joy, peace and so on, as well as acts of kindness and a pure life—were themselves signs that the Holy Spirit was at work in the individual's life. This in turn was evidence of justification, which revealed an effective call and election.

It is not difficult to see that such a sifting is fraught with problems. Sensitive souls would find it difficult to decide if their life was changed enough or holy enough to lead to the conclusion of election, and at the other extreme the possibility of pride and a severe judgment of others became a distinct possibility. Coolidge eloquently describes the practice of self-scrutiny as 'like straining every nerve in an effort to relax.'[17] John Stachniewski has examined the psychological and social effects of predestination and the doctrine of assurance in detail, showing that this teaching was far from theoretical and had far-reaching and often tragic consequences.[18]

## Pastoral Theology: Dealing with the Anxious and Uncertain

Hearing the doctrines of certainty and assurance, of election and firm faith preached had, we know, pastoral repercussions. In the latter part of the sixteenth century a ministry developed that was focused upon reassuring those who were anxious and troubled. One man who dealt with this on a regular basis was the Rev'd Richard Greenham. Greenham was a parish priest in Dry Drayton, Cambridge and seems to have acted in many ways like a present-day spiritual director. In their biography of him, Parker and Colson write of a pastoral ministry dedicated to the cure of afflicted consciences.[19] On paper the tension between doubt and faith, between certainty and confusion, between temporary and false faith and weak faith was complex, but even more so when read by and into the lives of those Christians who had taken to heart the demand to examine themselves and were left unsure as to how to read their lives in the light of the teaching. This was no theoretical debate; it had real and serious consequences for many, and very much in the here and now.

**This debate had real and serious consequences for many**

When coupled with teaching on predestination the doctrine of assurance could leave in its wake a fearful and fragile congregation. It was these very souls who flocked to Greenham for counsel. He was known to practice a holistic theology that took seriously mind, body and spirit—often counselling people to eat well as part of a holy life, and not simply to pray more!

So how did he engage with the anxiety and questions raised by the teaching on assurance and certainty? In many ways it was simple. Greenham was a believer in the *ordo salutis* and saw this as the source of comfort and truth regarding salvation it was no doubt intended to be. But he then takes an interesting turn. For him, evidence of being on that pathway, of being part of the elect, was simply shown by the act of coming to see him.

> In case after case his student reported that Greenham began with a reminder that the very fact they sought spiritual counsel was a sign of the Holy Spirit working in their life and evidence of grace.[20]

He taught the same need to sift lives for evidence, but saw his role as building the confidence of those who came, so that they would be sure in their election, through teaching, fellowship and a rhythm of life—good spiritual habits. They would then examine their lives with a clearer vision of God's presence and grace. Doubt and fear were signs of weak and not reprobate faith and so their faith simply needed to be strengthened through good discipline, grounded upon the confidence he had persuaded them to have.[21]

Alongside Greenham other clergy and theologians were exploring this area and taking seriously the pastoral implications. One of them was Richard Hooker.

# 3 Exploring Richard Hooker

## Who is Richard Hooker and Why Should We Draw Him into the Conversation?

Richard Hooker was born in 1554, right in the middle of the century we have been exploring. In 1579 he was ordained in the Church of England alongside his role of Professor of Hebrew at Corpus Christi College, Oxford. However, he only comes to public attention when he takes up the post of Master of the Temple Church in London in 1585. (Master is just the title given to the priest in charge of this particular church.) You may have come across the Temple Church as it features in Dan Brown's *Da Vinci Code*, or you may have visited this architecturally interesting church on a visit to London. It was bombed during the Second World War and has been restored, but it still has a plaque to Hooker. It is nestled amidst the Inns of Court and across from the Royal Courts of Justice.

What brings Hooker to the attention of the church hierarchy is a very public argument with his Reader, Walter Travers. Being a Reader in the sixteenth century is not the same as being a Reader now. This was not a lay position, a type of local preacher. Travers was also ordained and importantly had been so on the continent where he had fled during the persecution under Queen Mary. Travers was described as a Puritan and a Presbyterian—a man who was looking for the church to reform itself further, to purify itself of anything that was inherited from or seemed to be like the Roman Catholic Church. This was not simply about theology; this was also about church structure and ministerial orders.

Travers and Hooker clashed, almost from the beginning of Hooker's time at the Temple. Both men were committed to the Reformation but their views on the structure of the church were always going to bring them into dispute. But what is fascinating is that they also clash on matters of theology, so much so that Travers brought his concerns to the Privy Council—the group of men who advised the monarch. This may seem strange to us, but was not as surprising then, although it was still a very serious thing to do.

One key issue for Travers was Hooker's sermons on certainty and assurance. And here we begin to discover just why Hooker may be an interesting person to draw into our discussion, for as he explored and engaged with these issues of assurance and certainty, his answer provides a very different approach from those we have already explored.

## Exploring Hooker's Views on Certainty

On the face of it, *A Learned and Comfortable Sermon of the Certaintie and Perpetuitie in the Elect* looks much like a regular Calvinist sermon, but as this is one of the sermons that caused Walter Travers to become concerned as to Hooker's reformed credentials, we are already on the alert to look out for what may be different here.

This sermon is the third in a series and sadly parts one and two are missing. If you get the chance to take a look at it, you may give thanks for not being a member of Hooker's congregation! It can be a little tricky to follow in places, and there is no sign of any personal story to reel the listener in or three points all starting with the same letter…but it is, nonetheless, fascinating, rich and evocative.

In this sermon Hooker is facing head on the question of the day: how is it possible for Christians to have a weak faith? If God's grace is within us, if we are 'taught of God' then how come our faith is often 'mingled with feare and wavering'?[22] This question, as we have seen, is not simply theoretical. If weak faith, the presence of doubts and fears, is not a possibility, then the reality would be that many who thought of themselves as Christian actually were not. Weak faith would, in effect, mean no faith.

Hooker does not leave this question hanging. His whole approach is one of affirmation and encouragement. The very people who have questions and doubts and even fears are described as those who have God's grace and are taught by God. The implication is that they are indeed Christian. Weak faith is not evidence of a lack of faith. But he immediately goes a step further. We treat doubt and questions, a lack of certainty about God, as a strange phenomenon, he says and that is where we have gone wrong. It is not strange; in fact it is expected and a natural part of faith. It is certainty that is neither possible nor desirable. Assurance and peace are available as Christians, but certainty is not.

**Assurance and peace are available as Christians, but certainty is not**

On what basis can Hooker say this? The remainder of the sermon sets out his answer.

## Disarming Doubt: Thinking about How We Know and How Certain Our Knowing Can Be

Hooker grapples with the question of weak faith by taking a step back. What he is interested in at the outset is how we know things at all. For faith is also about knowing. Faith, he says, is made up of two different sorts of knowing: a knowing of the mind (evidential certainty) and a knowing of the heart (the certainty of adherence). Thomas Aquinas had used these same categories, so this was not new and many of his learned congregation may have been aware of this. But Aquinas, a medieval Catholic theologian, was not always widely used by the Reformers, and his hearers might have found Hooker's use of them intriguing. Indeed, what he does with these categories creates a very different picture from either Aquinas or Hooker's fellow Reformers.

## Certainty of Evidence

> Certainty of evidence wee call that, when the mind doth assent unto this or that, not because it is true in it selfe, but because the truth therof is cleere, because it is manifest to us.[23]

In this first category Hooker is considering the more usual way that we know, for example through sight or by logic. This is where the truth is so self-evident that all but the foolish would agree, and he gives as an example the statement that a part is less than the whole. This seems straightforward. But our certainty, he says, flows not from the nature of what is being proven but from the fact that we can grasp the truth of this by our minds.

Now, he says, the truths of the Christian faith are also true in themselves, in fact they are 'more certayn then any science' but these truths cannot be infallibly proven to us evidentially, and we know this because not all of us have equal certainty about matters of faith.[24] Those different levels of certainty are not because of sin or lack of faith, but because evidential certainty cannot deliver certainty to us in matters of faith. The truth about God will never seem as certain to us as our knowing that 2+2=4. This does not make God any less certain in Godself or the things of God any less certain, we just cannot know them fully in this way by logic or sight or so on. It follows—and this is crucial—that we should not expect to have this kind of certainty. This, he adds, is not because we are sinful or not very bright; this is because God is God and we can never know God in the same way that we can know that this is a table or the result of a mathematical equation. God is not one other thing to be known in this world. 'I conclud therefore that wee have less certaintie of evidence concerning things beleeved than concerning things sensibly or naturally perceived.'[25]

This may seem like simple logic and we may wonder what all the fuss is about but, for Travers (and he is not alone here) Hooker's teaching was dangerous. Hooker was, he said, denigrating faith—making it *less* certain than that which we reason or see. Travers wants to say that faith is *more* certain. He wanted to argue that the assurance of faith was *more than* and not *less than* this type of certainty.

Travers takes his concerns to the highest level, petitioning the Privy Council, exclaiming that Hooker had taught, 'the assurance of that we beleeve by the word, is not so certeyne as of that we percyve by sense.'[26]

Hooker's reply seems to have the tone of incredulity. Of course, he says, the things of God are more certain in themselves. It is simply that we cannot see that, we cannot know that in the same way that we know other things. It is obvious that this sort of evidential certainty feels more sure and certain and it is also obvious that we do not all seem to have the same degree of certainty about matters of faith, whereas when we look at the moon we all agree it is the moon.[27]

Hooker is not saying that there is no evidence for the Christian faith, but that it is not a full and certain evidence. The point for Hooker is that if we fool ourselves that faith should feel the same as knowing that this is a table then we are always going to think that we have a weak faith, or we are going to pretend to a certainty that is not there (and which, he is arguing, could not be there). But the truth is that we are approaching the question from the wrong angle. We should not be comparing how we know 2+2=4 with how we know God. By doing this we are comparing apples and chairs, and once we realize this, we can see that the sort of doubt that arises from lack of evidential certainty is normal and so we can take it in our stride.[28]

**Hooker declares that there might be more evidence against faith**

What becomes more problematic is what comes later, when Hooker declares that evidential certainty for faith is not always simply less, but that there might be more evidence against faith. But that claim is woven in with his exploration of the second type of knowing—that of adherence.

## Certainty of Adherence

It is striking that when Hooker defined the certainty of evidence, he wrote about the mind but when he turns to the certainty of adherence Hooker writes of the heart. 'The other which wee call the certaintie of adherence is when the hart doth cleeve and stick unto that which it doth beleeve.'[29] The certainty delivered by 'heart' faith 'is greater in us than the other.'[30] The certainty of adherence delivers a greater certainty than the certainty of evidence.

Before we can start to explore why this certainty is greater, we need first to ascertain what Hooker means by 'adherence.' He describes the heart 'cleaving and sticking' to that which we believe. His choice of words is evocative and suggests much more than mental assent (which is why, I think, he used the heart here and not the mind). Cleaving would resonate immediately with his listeners, reminding them of Genesis 2 and the description of the husband cleaving to his wife. This is a word used of relationships, with hints of passionate embrace, of desire and vow. Whilst 'stick' does not have the same sensual undertones it adds into the mix a sense of resolve; a binding that determinedly clings on.

Adherence, it seems, takes on a much more sensual air. This is not about logic and reason, but about desire and resolve.

But there is a crucial question still to be answered. Why does the heart hold onto that which is believed? We need to pause here a moment as what comes next is of infinite importance. When Hooker spoke of evidential certainty this seemed to be about fact, about truth as propositional. But as he explores this other way of knowing, which he argues is key to Christian faith, he goes further than truth. That which is believed, he says, is not only true but good. God is not only true but good. And God's promises towards us are good. 'The fayth of a christian man doth apprehend the wordes of the law, the promises of god, not only as true but also as good.'[31]

**Why does the heart hold onto that which is believed?**

This experience of the truth and goodness of God is what makes us cleave and stick to God. But how do we know that God and God's promises are good? Hooker's response might well be food for thought for John Humphreys and others like him, and what follows is brutally honest and challenging. We do not always know God's goodness through evidential certainty—in fact the evidence can be quite to the contrary or can be very small indeed. We may find this hard to admit, he says, but we must if we are to be honest. In the face of evil and suffering, the evidence of our eyes, reason can hardly find a foothold to believe that God is good. Hooker writes of 'when the evidence which he hath of the trueth is so small that it greaveth him to feel his weaknes in assenting thereunto.'[32]

If the evidence is so small, what makes us continue believing? Is this simply self-delusion? No, says Hooker. The delusion comes from pretending otherwise. We need to acknowledge the awfulness of what we see. But faith does not stop here. Even then 'is there in him such a sure adherence unto that which he doth but faintly and fearfully beleeve' that the evidence of our eyes and reason does not remove our faith.[33] Why? Hooker's answer is not about evidence and argument—about what will sway our intellects. Nor is it about will and decision—about a need to somehow make ourselves more certain than we currently feel. Instead, it is more sensual. Once we have truly tasted the goodness of God, he says, 'the heavenly sweetnes,' this is enough to make us hang on, even against all the evidence of our eyes and our mind.[34] Truth and goodness are woven together in faith, and it is the taste of goodness that allows us to hold on even when the evidential certainty seems low. Here is Hooker at his most poetic and pastoral, capturing the wrestling of faith and the agony of believing:

> all the world is not able quite and cleane to remove him from it but striveth with him selfe to hope even against hope to beleeve even against all reason of believing, being settled with Job upon this unmoveable resolution, *though god shall slay me I will not geve over trusting in him.* For why? this lesson remayneth for ever imprinted in his hart, *it is good for me to cleve unto god.*[35]

This is a beautiful description of faith. This tasting of God's goodness leaves within the heart an imprint, that tells us that it is good to cleave to God (not just the right thing to do). How many times have we remembered the taste of something in such a way that although it is a memory it is as if we can taste it now? Or the way that a smell can evoke memories, bringing into the present the reality of the past? This sensuous way of knowing is real for us as embodied human beings, and what we now know that Hooker did not is the huge interweaving between our minds, bodies and spirits.[36]

## But is this Just a Different Type of Certainty (but Still Certainty)?

It is true that Hooker speaks of certainty both in connection with evidence and adherence. Whilst we cannot expect evidential certainty it seems that we can expect the certainty of adherence. So maybe this is not that different after all to what had been said before?

Except that is not quite what Hooker says. His argument is that adherence delivers a greater degree of certainty, but still not full certainty. And the language he uses is crucially important here. Hooker knows that, for some, what he has already said will bring comfort: a recognition that doubt in both areas is to be expected so it need not lead to despair. When we turn to adherence, this certainty, which exceeds evidential certainty, still does not sound robust, triumphalistic and loudly confident. This is not a self-assured declaration of a felt faith, but rather an almost gentle admission of a personal experience of God's goodness, that does not lead to a convinced declaration but rather an inner wrestling. This sounds like a very different tone from the usual sixteenth century sermons.

As the sermon continues, Hooker delves into the complex area of sin. Whilst some of our doubts are not a surprise, some of them do come from sinfulness. And even then, he wants to nuance this further to include doubting through infidelity and doubting through infirmity—but how do we know the difference? Is not this the nub of the problem, even if Hooker has introduced a more nuanced understanding of faith?

## How Do We Know when Doubt is a Sign of Unbelief?

The final section of the sermon deals with Hooker's fourth question, which is focussed on a short text from Habbakuk, the basis of his sermon. At first sight this text seems rather obscure and not at all inspiring:

> So the law becomes slack and justice never prevails.
> The wicked surround the righteous—
> therefore judgment comes forth perverted.
>
> Hab 1.4[37]

The question, says Hooker, is whether by saying this, Habbakuk showed himself to be an unbeliever.[38] Hooker is now facing the question that has been in the background: how do we differentiate and discern between doubts that are weak faith and those that are signs of reprobation? What if those who are despairing look at the world around them and say, 'Actually, I'm not sure whether God is good. Just look at X, how can we believe that the promises of God are true and good when "bad things happen to good people" or the innocent? Is not this the cry of John Humphreys and folk like him? It is not just about the evidence, it is about something in our gut. Some people seem to be able to dig deep and find faith even in the face of the "evidence" and you, Hooker, have said this is because they have tasted God's goodness. Well, I have looked, and I can't find that. I am indeed faithless.'[39]

Hooker takes this seriously. It is no good, he says, building with pearl if we build on stubble and it all comes falling down.[40] This is surely an allusion to the golden chain of salvation we looked at earlier. It is a wonderful doctrine, once you are in the circle, but if you do not think you are in, or no longer in, then it does not matter how wonderful it is because it will not deliver the comfort and assurance that was intended.

Hooker takes these people with him to listen to Habbakuk, who is declaring that God's justice is not evident in the world around him. Habbakuk can see no sign of God. God is not there. The law has failed. God is not keeping his promises; God is not good and cannot be trusted.

Hooker then declares that Habbakuk's faith has not failed, and so neither has theirs. And he is going to show them why.[41]

Hooker begins by speaking of the agony that many go through who think they have lost their faith. He calls it an 'extremity of grief' and describes how they lament for what they cannot find.[42] These are broken people and he 'dare not for their sakes deal slightly in this cause.'[43]

Hooker goes on to think carefully about what can lead to this, and with great foresight he speaks first of illness. Sometimes, he says, you think you do not have faith because you are not well. Hooker calls it 'a melingcholie passion proceeding only from that dejection of minde the cause whereof is in the body and by bodily meanes maie be taken away.'[44] There are echoes here of Greenham, urging his visitors to eat well and exercise.

However, if there is no physical cause then he thinks there are three possibilities. First, we compare ourselves with others and find ourselves wanting; or we look back and see our own faith as having been much stronger in the past. Neither of these are helpful, he says but these comparisons may show a weaker faith, but not an absence of faith.[45]

Secondly, we believe that we should be joyful, and when joy is not present, we think this is a sign of lack of faith.[46] It is here that we start to see that when Hooker is speaking of the tasting of God as good, he is referring to more than feeling. There are many reasons why we do not feel joy, and again these times can help us to appreciate joy when it is present rather than being signs of a lack of faith. In fact, he says, too much joy can be bad for us; it can make us puffed up and complacent. We may not want to agree with Hooker totally here. The idea that God sends bad times to help us to appreciate the good ones, to teach us things, is poor and dangerous theology. However, there is a sense in which Hooker is not really saying that; he is more concerned with those who flaunt the good times as something to be proud of, who become puffed up with their own good lives and become complacent and judgmental. He wants to encourage those for whom the 'dark night of the soul' has arrived, that this is not a godless place, it is a place where God is with them and the grief they feel is not evidence of a lack of faith.

**God is with them—the grief they feel is not evidence of a lack of faith**

And thirdly, there are those who have honestly looked at their inner lives and know that they are not pure. He says they 'fasten their cogitations upon the distrustfull suggestions of the flesh' which they find in abundance in themselves.[47] They are impure, and believe that they would not be if they had faith. This is not true, he says. Your faith is buried beneath these overwhelmings, but it is there and God hears the groans of your spirit as prayer.

Hooker knows that whilst there are some who have taken comfort from this, there is still a small group who say, 'Yes, I have heard all of that but I am still not comforted because I have sifted all that you have said and yet I know I do not believe.' This surely is the strongest evidence and even Hooker cannot refute this. Here is the one who knows that whilst he may have once had faith, he has no longer. Well, says Hooker, I will take you at your word—and surely here he is defeated…but no, he has one more question to ask.

How do you feel about not having faith? He is now speaking to those for whom this is a source of grief and fear. 'Be it that they are faithless and without beliefe. But are they not greeved with ther unbeleefe?'[48] They are. These are people who are not flaunting their atheism like a weapon; these are people who look at the world and themselves and just cannot believe in a good God whose words are true and can be trusted.

Hooker now takes them by the hand and, surprisingly, leads them deeper into the darkness. 'Why do you grieve?' he asks. His argument is that we only grieve for what we love. We grieve because we wish it could be different.[49] Now Hooker does some interesting thinking, and we need to stay with him as this is quite complex. His argument is that they grieve because they have a secret love and liking for those very things they feel they do not believe in. That secret love reveals that they do in fact believe that these things exist. We could never love something that we believed did not exist. That secret love, that desiring, is in fact a sign of faith itself and not a sign that there is no faith. Faith, the gift of God, is discovered not in the certainty of faith but in the very desire to believe that the things of faith are true.

**Faith is discovered in the very desire to believe that the things of faith are true**

This is mind-blowing. Hooker has discovered the gift of faith in the darkest of places: in grief and turmoil. The gift of faith is not, here, a healthy and robust confidence but a fragile, hidden, lamenting desire.

This is not, of course, any sort of argument for the existence of God. Hooker is not concerned with that. That is, for him, a given. He is concerned with the comfort of the fearful. And in the end, this is not simply about their own salvation. Habbakuk's lament is not that he worries for his own eternal soul. No, he is worried about the character of God. And that, says Hooker, is often at the root of our doubts and weakness of faith. But it is in that very honest lament, in that realistic looking at the world as it is, in the reality of crying out to an absent God and not simply cheering each other up by repeating that

God is good or pretending that things are not as they are—it is here that the gift of faith is to be discovered, and where there is the gift there is the giver. Right there. In the godless place.

# 4 Conclusion

At the very beginning I posed two questions: how certain does Christian faith need to be, and is doubt the enemy of faith? The exploration of the question has showed that for some, both today and in the past, there is a need for certainty and assurance: Christians can indeed be sure of their beliefs and doubt is the enemy to be driven out.

But Richard Hooker led us into a different arena, one where he demonstrated that certainty is neither required of us nor even possible, for a variety of reasons—whether that is intellectual, evidential certainty or the more sensual, experiential assurance, which he calls adherence. In fact, he begins to hint that it is God who sticks to us, rather than us to God, in and through an encounter of tasting God's goodness that we can never quite rid ourselves of. He even suggests that certainty, rather than doubt, might be the enemy of faith.

This is a very different approach indeed. Is Hooker saying that what we believe does not matter? That Christian doctrine and learning is irrelevant? This would be an odd conclusion to draw when we consider the whole of Hooker's writing, in which he is pleading for Christians to become more and not less acquainted with Christian teaching. So what is he saying?

**Hooker is setting out the limits of theology and the purpose of doctrine**

He is setting out, I think, the limits of theology and the purpose of doctrine. The aim of learning is not to arrive at certainty; our experience of God is not one that will lead to certainty. Our knowledge—of both kinds—is to lead us further into glimpsing who God is, this God who saves us. Those glimpses will sometimes be like blinding lights but at times they may well lead us to doubt and darkness. Both paths can lead us deeper into God, revealing to us more of God's goodness and more of the God who takes hold of us in salvation. Belief and doubt can lead us into an honest faith that allows us to believe in God with integrity.

More people than we realize have serious questions about the Christian faith and God, not just outside the church, but inside. Many may not dare to utter them for fear of being branded as unbelievers. Maybe Hooker brings a different perspective to this. Maybe his insight could open up space in our lives together to share our questions and concerns about God honestly, assured that they point towards and not away from the God we desire.

# Appendix: Reading Hooker

## What Did He Write?

Hooker wrote only one book, *The Lawes of Ecclesiastical Polity,* but it is in eight volumes (confusingly called books). Five of these books were published in his lifetime and three after his death. Alongside this book are sermons, some notes, and also texts that are connected to various controversies and arguments that involved him. These give us a fascinating insight into his theology.

It has to be said at the outset that Hooker is not easy to read! His work is still in sixteenth-century language with all its odd spellings, and that can be a hurdle for many. For those who manage to cope with this the challenges continue, for Hooker's style is not for the faint-hearted. Whilst many applaud his language others despair. He is famous for writing very long sentences. For example in Book One of the *Lawes* it has been noted that his sentences range from 2 to 267 words and that, of the 723 sentences, 302 are long (40 words and over) and 71 are very long (80 words and over).[50]

He also enjoys building complex arguments, looking at issues from one side and then another and more than one scholar has found himself misunderstanding whether Hooker is building his own argument or describing that of his opponent.

It may seem odd for someone as passionate as I am about Hooker to say all of this. However, if we read texts on Hooker that expound his beautiful prose and fluent arguments it can then come as a shock to the reader if, having been inspired to open the pages of the *Lawes,* we are met with some of the challenges I have outlined. Forewarned is forearmed! With a few tips on how to read Hooker there is a wealth of rich thought and challenging theology ahead.

## Tips on Reading Hooker

An online version of the *Lawes* is available in which the spelling has been changed to modern spelling, so many people find this a great help. The version is that of John Keble in the nineteenth century (you will discover that there are various versions available):
https://oll.libertyfund.org/titles/hooker-the-works-of-richard-hooker-vol-1

Brad Littlejohn is also releasing an Everyman series, seeking to provide a summary of sections of the *Lawes* in order to widen the readership. You can find details about this here:
https://bradlittlejohn.com/category/richard-hooker/everymans-hooker/

Over the years I have also found a few ways that have helped me read this complex prose and so I am sharing them with you and I hope that they help.

Here are my top tips for reading Hooker:

- Read it out loud.
- Read it in a group (also out loud!).
- Read a good-sized section and read it three times. The first time it will make little sense. On the second read, read slowly and make notes if that helps. Reading in a group will mean that you will be able to ask questions of each other. On the third read it will start to gel.
- Do not get too bogged down. Just keep reading and eventually both the spelling and the way of writing starts to make sense. You even begin to appreciate the beauty and the rhythm of the writing, and this adds to and illuminates the content.

# Notes

1 A Thiselton, *Doubt, Faith and Certainty* (Grand Rapids, MI: Eerdmans, 2017); G Ward, *Unbelievable: Why We Believe and Why We Don't* (London: L B Tauris and Co Ltd, 2014); A Wright, *Exploring Doubt: Landscapes of Loss and Longing* (London: Darton, Longman and Todd, 2017).

2 D Tomlinson, *Black Sheep and Prodigals: An Antidote to Black and White Religion* (London: Hodder and Stoughton, 2017).

3 I Paul, 'Should faith be certain?' *Psephizo,* 26 April 2017, accessed 27 October 2020, https://www.psephizo.com/life-ministry/should-faith-be-certain/

4 J Humphreys, *In God We Doubt: Confessions of a Failed Atheist* (London: Hodder and Stoughton, 2007).

5 D K Shuger, 'Faith and Assurance,' in W J T Kirby (ed), *A Companion to Richard Hooker* (Leiden: Brill, 2008) p 224.

6 D K Shuger, 'Faith and Assurance,' *op cit,* p 223, quoting from Melanchthon, *Romerbrief-Kommentar* 1532 (her translation).

7 NRSV.

8 A Maxey, *The Golden Chaine of Mans Salvation* (London, 1610).

9 D D Wallace Jr, *Puritans and Predestination: Grace in English Protestant Theology 1525–1695* (Chapel Hill, NC: The University of North Carolina Press, 1982) p 46.

10 J Calvin, J T NcNeill (ed), *Institutes of the Christian Religion*, F L Battles (trans), (Philadelphia, PA: The Westminster Press, 1960) vol 1, p 543.

11 Calvin, *Institutes, op cit,* 1.549.

12 Calvin, *Institutes, op cit,* 1.560 and 1.564.

13 Calvin, *Institutes, op cit,* 1.560.

14 Calvin, *Institutes, op cit,* 1.587.

15 Calvin, *Institutes, op cit,* 1.587.

16 Calvin, *Institutes, op cit,* 1.555.

17 JCoolidge, *The Pauline Renaissance in England* (Oxford: Clarendon Press, 1970) p 132.

18 J Stachniewski, *The Persecutory Imagination: English Puritanism and the Literature of Religious Despair* (Oxford: Clarendon Press, 1991) p 1.

19 K L Parker and E J Carlson, *'Practical Divinity': The Works and Life of Revd Richard Greenham* (Aldershot: Routledge, 1998).

20 Parker and Coulson, *Practical Divinity, op cit*, p 90.

21 Parker and Coulson, *Practical Divinity, op cit*, chapters 6 and 7.

22 R Hooker, W S Hill (Ed), *The Folger Library Edition of the Works of Richard Hooker*, VII vols (I-V, Cambridge, MA: 1977–1990; VI, Birmingham, NY: 1993; VII, Tempe, AZ: 1998). The edition of Hooker's works I am using is The Folger Library Edi-

tion of the Works of Richard Hooker. These volumes are referenced in a certain way—by putting the volume number first, then page and then line number. This reference is to be found here: V.69.20.

**23** Hooker, *FLE, op cit*, V.70.1.

**24** Hooker, *FLE, op cit*, V.69.24.

**25** Hooker, *FLE, op cit*, V.70.23.

**26** Travers, *A Supplication made to the Privy Counsel by Master Walter Travers*, in *Folger*, *op cit*, V.189–210.

**27** Hooker, *Answer: Master Hookers Answer to the Supplication that Master Travers made to the Counsell, FLE, op cit*, V.236.30.

**28** Hooker, *FLE, op cit*, V.70.

**29** Hooker, *FLE, op cit*, V.70.31.

**30** Hooker, *FLE, op cit*, V.71.1.

**31** Hooker, *FLE, op cit*, V.71.3.

**32** Hooker, *FLE, op cit*, V.71.5.

**33** Hooker, *FLE, op cit*, V.71.8.

**34** Hooker, *FLE, op cit*, V.71.9.

**35** Hooker, *FLE, op cit*, V.71.9–15.

**36** And for those who know him as the champion of the reason, this may come as quite a surprise.

**37** Hooker, *FLE, op cit*, V.69.4.

**38** Hooker, *FLE, op cit*, V.73.11.

**39** Hooker, *FLE, op cit*, V.73–74.

**40** Hooker, *FLE, op cit*, V.73.19.

**41** Hooker, *FLE, op cit*, V.73.25.

**42** Hooker, *FLE, op cit*, V.74.14.

**43** Hooker, *FLE, op cit*, V.74.11.

**44** Hooker, *FLE, op cit*, V.74.23.

**45** Hooker, *FLE, op cit*, V.74.25.

**46** Hooker, *FLE, op cit*, V.74.29 onwards.

**47** Hooker, *FLE, op cit*, V.75.20

**48** Hooker, *FLE, op cit*, V.76.8

**49** Hooker, *FLE, op cit*, V.76 onwards.

**50** Georges Edelen, 'Hooker's Style,' in W S Hill (ed), *Studies in Richard Hooker: Essays Preliminary to an Edition of His Works* (Cleveland and London: Case Western Reserve University Press, 1972) pp 251, 241.